Children's FIRST Book of SCIENCE

Children's FIRST Book of SCIENCE

•PARRAGON•

Author and Editor
Neil Morris

Projects created by
Ting Morris

Art Direction
Full Steam Ahead Ltd

Designer
Branka Surla

Project Management
Rosie Alexander

Artwork commissioned by
Branka Surla

Picture Research
Rosie Alexander, Kate Miles, Elaine Willis, Yannick Yago

Editorial Assistant
Lynne French

Additional editorial help from
Hilary Bird, Jenny Sharman

Editorial Director
Jim Miles

The publishers would like to thank the following people for their help:
Suzanne Airey, Jenni Cozens, Pat Crisp

First published in 1998

This edition published in 1999 by Parragon

Parragon
Queen Street House, 4 Queen Street,
Bath BA1 1HE

2468109753

Produced by Miles Kelly Publishing Ltd
Bardfield Centre, Great Bardfield, Essex CM7 4SL

ISBN 0-75253-253-7

Printed in Italy

Contents

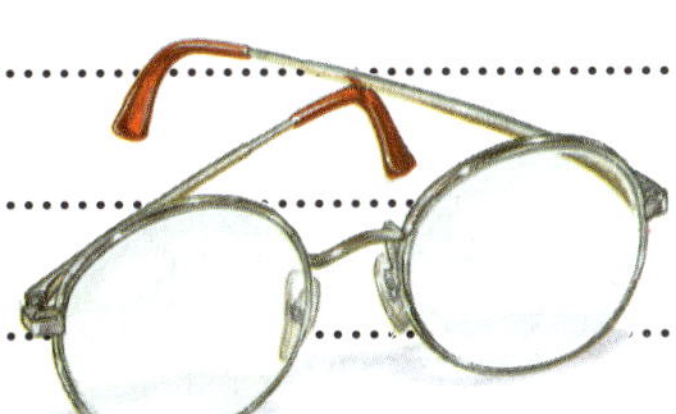

How to use this book

In this book, every page is filled with information on the sort of topics that you will enjoy reading about.

Information is given in photographs and illustrations, as well as in words. All the pictures are explained by captions, to tell you what you are looking at and to give even more detailed facts.

Caption triangles point to the right picture. Other captions starting with a symbol give extra pieces of information that you will find interesting.

Illustrations are clear and simple, and sometimes they are cut away so that you can see inside things.

The cartoons throughout the book are not always meant to be taken too seriously! They are supposed to be fun, but the text that goes with them gives real information.

Project boxes describe craft activities related to the topic. These are things to make or simple experiments to do. The photograph helps to show you what to do, and is there to inspire you to have a go! But remember, some of the activities can be quite messy, so put old newspaper down first. Always use round-ended scissors, and ask an adult for help if you are unsure of something or need sharp tools or materials.

The main text on each double-page spread gives a short introduction to that particular topic. Every time you turn the page, you will find a new topic.

A New Words box appears on every double-page spread. This list explains some difficult words and technical terms.

Beautiful photographs have been specially chosen to bring each subject to life. The caption triangle points to the right photograph.

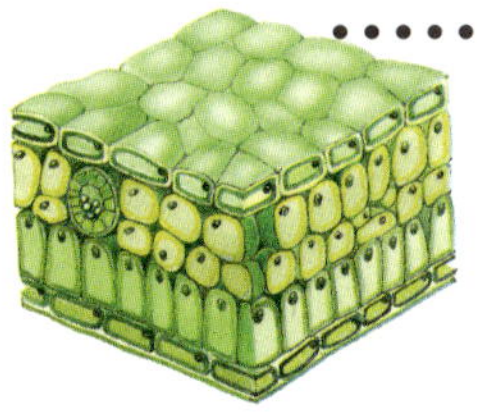

Science

Science is an exciting way of finding out about the world around us. What are things made of? How can we measure time? How do things work and why do they work the way they do?

Scientists have been asking and trying to answer fascinating questions such as these and many others for thousands of years. They have invented machines to help them and make life easier. In recent times, television and the computer have changed the way many people live and work. Yet plants are just the same as they were centuries ago, and there is still a lot to learn about them, too. Science is knowledge, and science is fun.

Finding Out

The word "science" really means knowledge. It is all about finding things out.

We can start finding out by looking at things very carefully. We can look at plants and animals, to see how they grow and change. We can look at rocks and fossils, to see how the Earth developed. We can look at the stars, to find out more about the Universe.

Scientists test things out, to see how they work. Their tests are called experiments, and they often involve measuring things. Scientists might measure size, weight or time.

△ **The best way to find out** about an animal and the way it behaves is to watch it carefully for some time. After watching, this boy could look up tortoises in an encyclopedia to find out more about them.

▽ **Science** helps our everyday lives. These researchers are using microscopes, computer images and chemicals to look for new medicines and help fight diseases.

Scientists look through microscopes so that they can see things close up. A microscope can make things look thousands of times bigger, so that you can see tiny details.

When scientists test things, they keep a note of their results. This could be in a notebook, although, today, scientists often use computers to record their information.

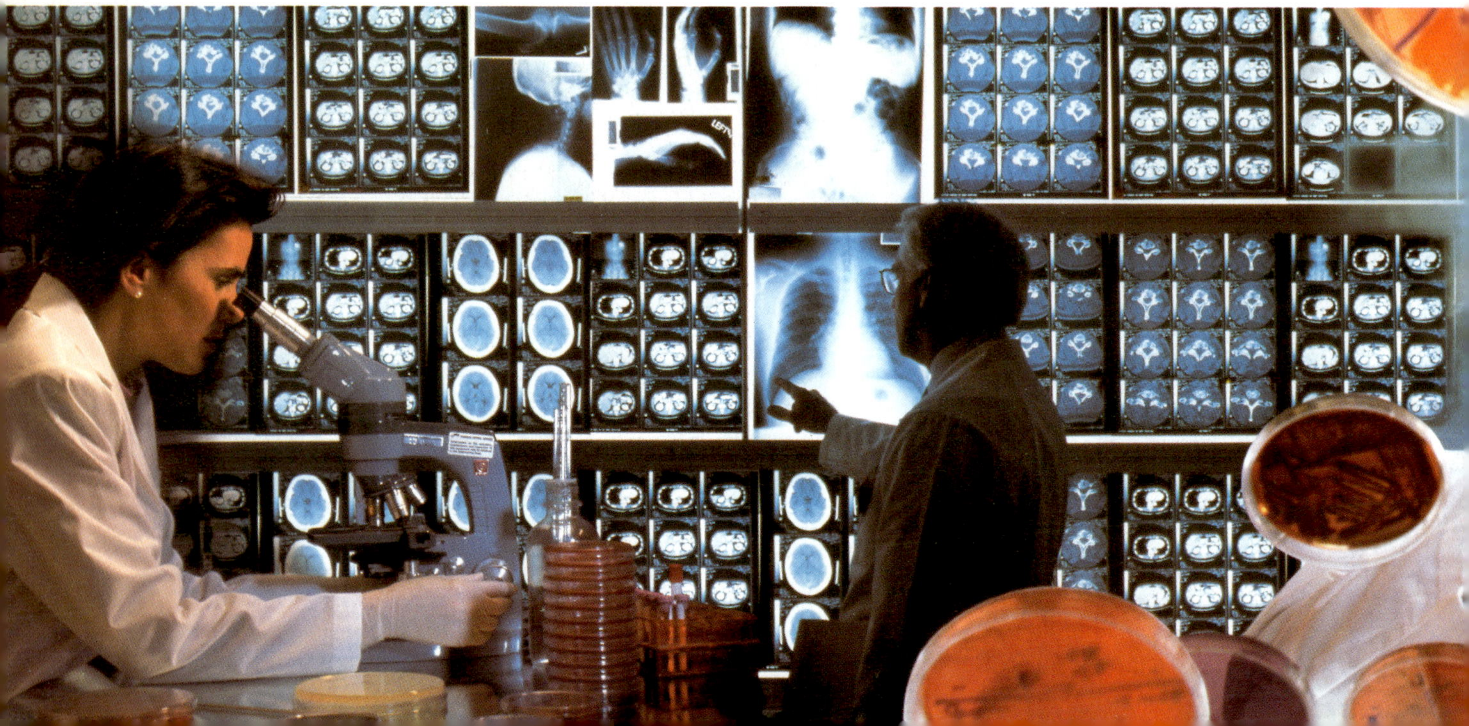

BEFORE AND AFTER

Try this simple experiment. Half-fill a measuring jug with water and note down the number of millilitres shown on the jug's scale. Then put your hand in the water and see how far the water rises. Again, note down the millilitres shown on the jug. Ask a friend to do the same, and compare your results.

▷ **A magnifying glass** is like a simple microscope. You can use one to see things more clearly and closer up. Through his magnifying glass, this boy can see the tiny markings on a caterpillar.

NEW WORDS

compact disk A piece of plastic that carries information for putting in a computer.

encyclopedia Books, like this one, or a compact disk containing information.

microscope An instrument that helps you see tiny details close up.

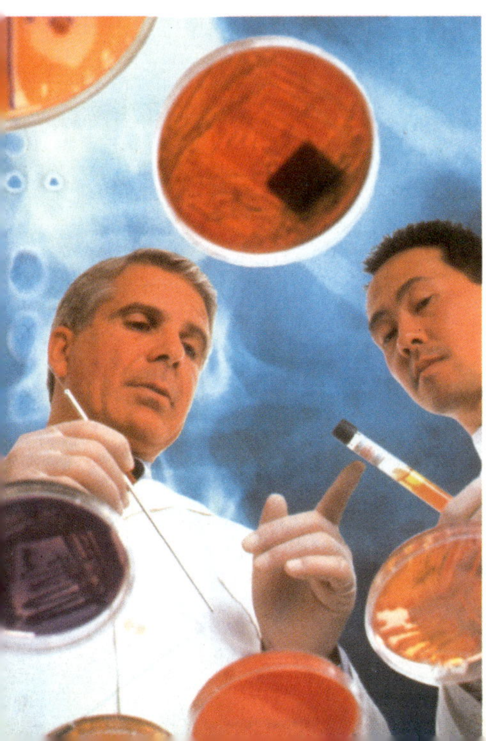

Time

When we are trying to find things out, time is very important. Scientists often need to measure how long it takes for things to happen.

The first clocks and calendars were invented thousands of years ago. They were based on the Earth's movements. We call one spin of the Earth a day. And we call the time it takes for the Earth to travel around the Sun a year. Our time is based on these movements.

▽ **The Earth** is divided into 24 time zones, one for each hour of the day. When it's 7 a.m. in New York City, USA, it's midday in London, UK, and already 9 p.m. in Tokyo, Japan.

△ **The sundial** is a type of shadow clock. The pointer's shadow moves around the dial as the Earth spins, pointing to the time. To us, it seems as if the Sun is moving across the sky.

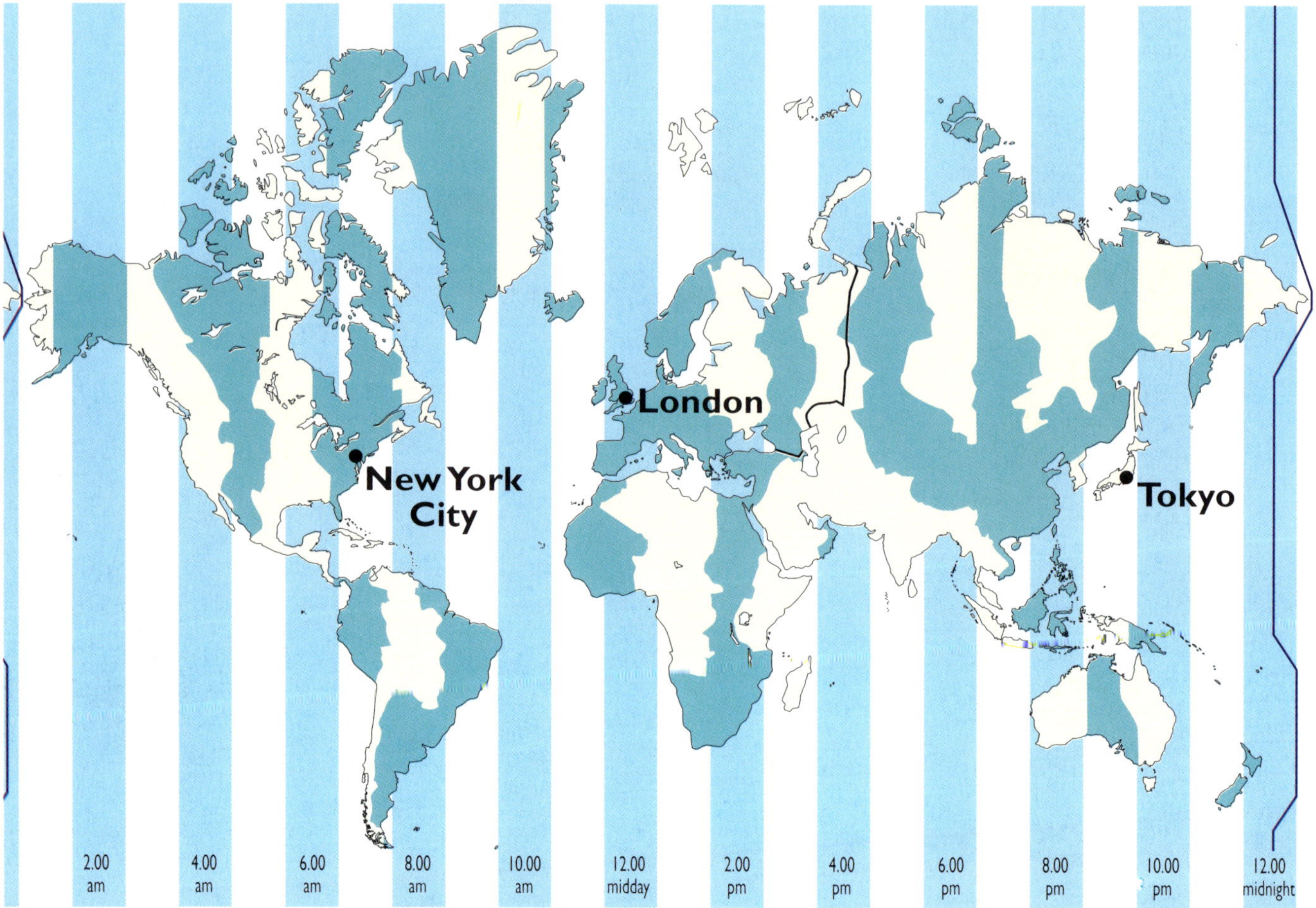

digital watch

candle clock

grandfather clock

pocket watch

▽ **The Earth** takes a year to travel around the Sun. We split this up into 12 calendar months of, usually, 30 or 31 days.

▽ **The Moon** makes 12 trips around the Earth during a year. These are called lunar months, but do not add up exactly to one year. Muslims keep to a lunar month.

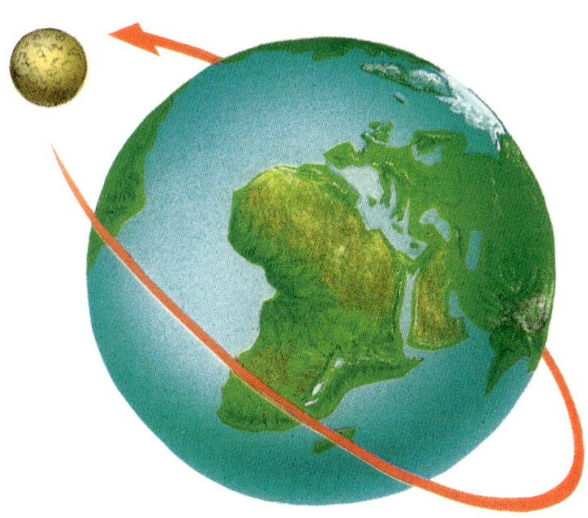

WATER CLOCK

Make a small hole in the bottom of a yoghurt pot. Attach a length of string to the pot and hang it up. Put another yoghurt pot under it. Then pour water into the hanging pot. Use a watch to time a minute and mark the water level on the bottom pot with a permanent marker. Carry on timing and marking more minutes. Then empty the bottom pot and refill the hanging pot. The marks on your water clock will now show you the passing minutes.

NEW WORDS

calendar A chart that shows us the days, weeks and months of the year.

Muslim To do with the religion of Muslim people, called Islam.

candle clock A candle marked to show the passing of hours.

Materials

We use all sorts of materials to make things. Different materials are used to do very different jobs.

Metals are strong and are good at standing heat. Plastics don't break easily and can have lots of different colours. Glass is useful to see through and looks good. Wood has been used by people for thousands of years. Today it is still used to make furniture, as well as paper for books and magazines.

Look around and see how many kinds of material you have in your home.

△ **Wood** can be carved into all sorts of different shapes. It is quite light, but it is also strong. Many things that used to be wood are now made of plastic.

▷ **Many toys** are made of plastic. They are light and don't break or chip easily. This makes them safe for young children to play with.

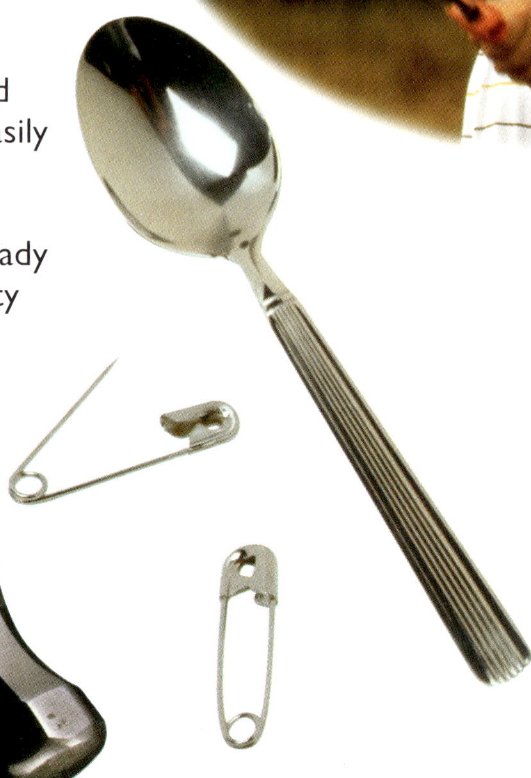

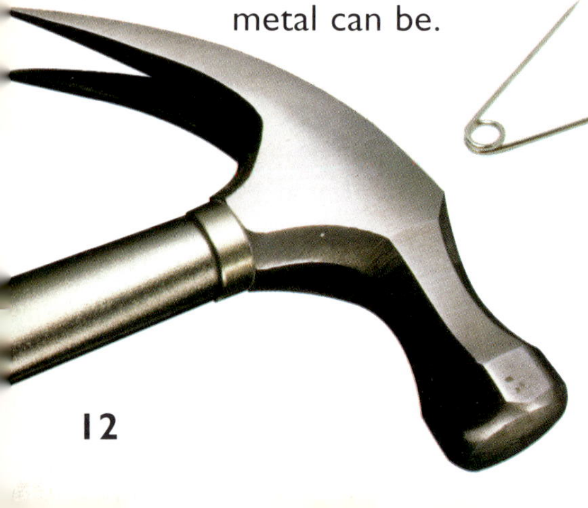

▽ **Metals** are hard and strong. A hammer would be of no use if it was easily knocked out of shape. Metal can also be sharpened to a point ready for piercing a hole. Safety pins show how useful metal can be.

What if?
In the story of Cinderella, she wears a glass slipper. But imagine really doing that – or trying to bash in nails with a glass hammer! You need to use the right materials for the job.

NEW WORDS

greenhouse A glass building used for growing plants.

plastic A man-made substance that can be moulded into a shape.

transparent That can be seen through.

▷ **Glass** is transparent – it lets light through. This makes it useful for drinks containers, because you can see what you are drinking. Light bulbs couldn't really be made of anything else!

◁ **The glass walls of a greenhouse** let the Sun's light and heat pass through. This is good for the plants inside. A wooden shed would keep out the light.

The first plastic was made by the American inventor John Wesley Hyatt, in 1868. It was called Celluloid. "Plastic" comes from a Greek word meaning "fit for moulding".

▷ **Plastics** can be moulded into all sorts of shapes. Most plastics will also bend quite easily. Many brushes are made entirely of this material.

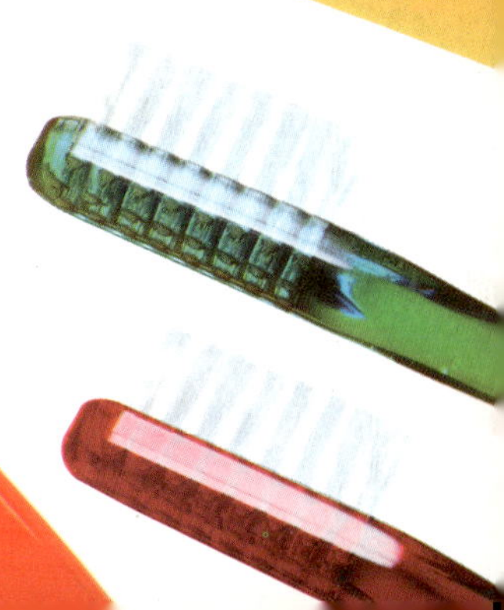

Solids, Liquids and Gases

Everything in the Universe, from the tiniest speck of dust to the biggest giant star, is made up of matter. This matter can take one of three forms: solid, liquid or gas.

A solid is a piece of matter that has a definite shape. Wood is a hard solid, and rubber is a soft solid. A liquid, such as water or lemonade, does not have a definite shape, but takes the shape of its container. A gas, such as air, also has no shape, and spreads out to fill any container it is put in.

△ **When a candle burns,** its solid wax gets hot, melts and goes liquid. As it cools, the wax goes hard again.

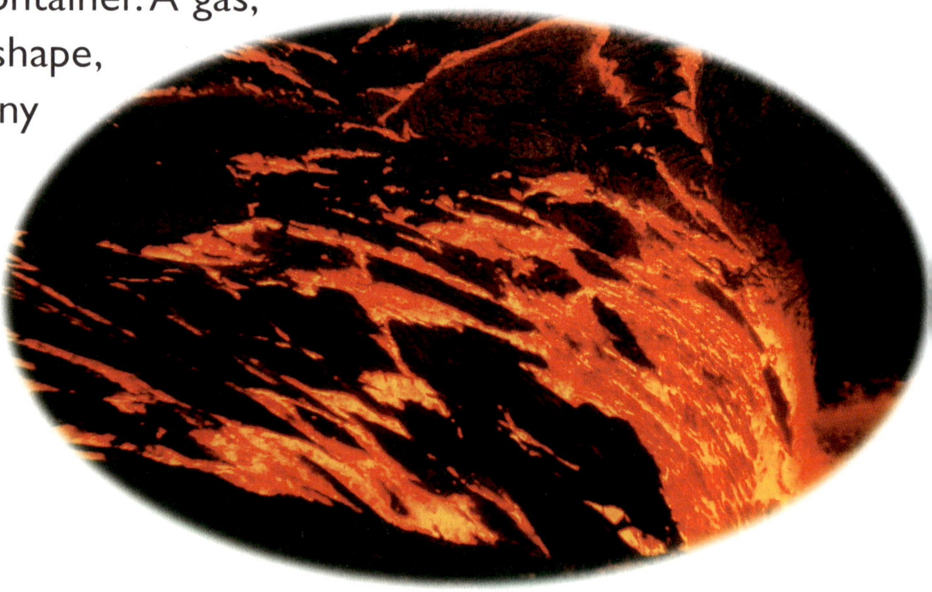

▷ **Red-hot lava** comes shooting out of a volcano as a liquid. The lava cools and turns into solid rock. Whether the lava is liquid or solid depends on its temperature. This is the same with candle wax.

▽ **Concrete** is shaped when it is runny, and then it hardens. A solid concrete building cannot turn into a liquid again.

▽ **A cake is baked** from a runny mixture, but you can't change it back again.

▽ **You can fry** a runny raw egg until it goes solid, but you can't unfry it!

▷ **Divers** take air underwater with them in cylinders strapped to their backs. If gas was let out of a cylinder, it would quickly bubble up to the surface. A pipe takes the air from a cylinder directly to a diver's mouth.

SLOW FREEZER

Salty water does not freeze as easily as fresh water. To test this, dissolve as much salt as you can in a tin-foil container of cold tap water. Then put this in the freezer, along with another container of cold tap water. You will find that the fresh water turns to solid ice much quicker than the salty water. This is because the salty water freezes at a much lower temperature.

Can water flow uphill?

No, water always flows downhill. This is because it is pulled by the force of gravity, just like everything else. Water settles at the lowest point it can reach.

NEW WORDS

concrete Cement mixed with sand and gravel, used in building.

dissolve To mix a solid into a liquid so that it becomes part of the liquid.

steam The very hot gas that boiling water turns into.

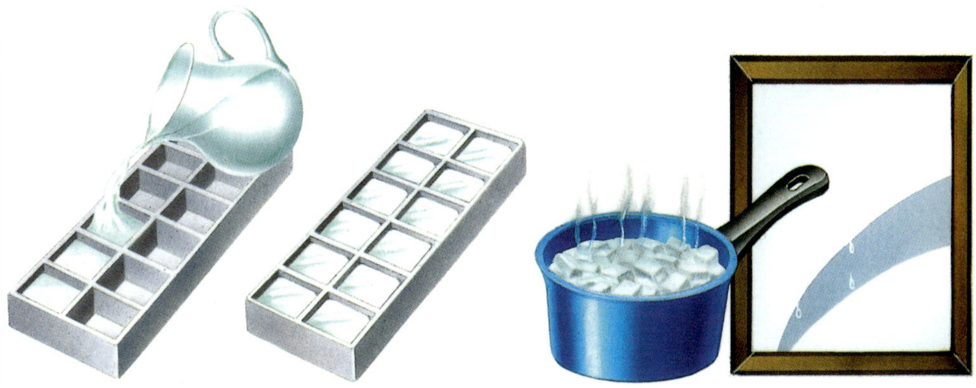

△ **If you pour water** into an ice tray and put it in the freezer, the liquid becomes solid ice. If you then heat the ice cubes, they become liquid again. When the water boils, it turns to a gas called steam. And when the steam cools on a mirror, it changes back to water!

All living things on Earth get their energy from the Sun. The food chain shows how we use the Sun's energy. Grass and other plants turn the Sun's rays into food, so they can grow. Cows eat grass and use its energy to make milk, which we collect. When we drink the milk, we can use its energy to work, play, run and jump!

▽ **The hot water in a radiator** warms the air, which in turn warms us. This movement of heat energy is called convection.

▽ **The Sun heats** the Earth and us by radiation. On a summer's day, it is best to stay in the shade and drink a lot to stay cool.

▽ **When you hold a hot mug,** the drink's heat passes through the mug and warms your hands. The mug is said to conduct heat.

Energy

All the world's actions and movements are caused by energy. Light, heat and electricity are all forms of energy. Our human energy comes from food.

Energy exists in many forms, and it always changes from one form to another. A car's energy comes from petrol. When it is burned in a car, it gives out heat energy. This turns into movement energy to make the car go. Many machines are powered in this way by fuel.

New Words

fuel Stored energy used to power machines.

petrol A liquid made from crude oil, used to power cars and other machines.

radiator A device in the home that gives off heat. It is often part of a central heating system.

▷ **Millions of years ago**, the remains of dead sea plants and animals were covered by mud and sand. Heat and pressure turned these into oil, which was trapped between rocks. We drill down to the oil and bring it to the surface. We make petrol from the oil, which we put into our cars. Then stored energy is turned into movement.

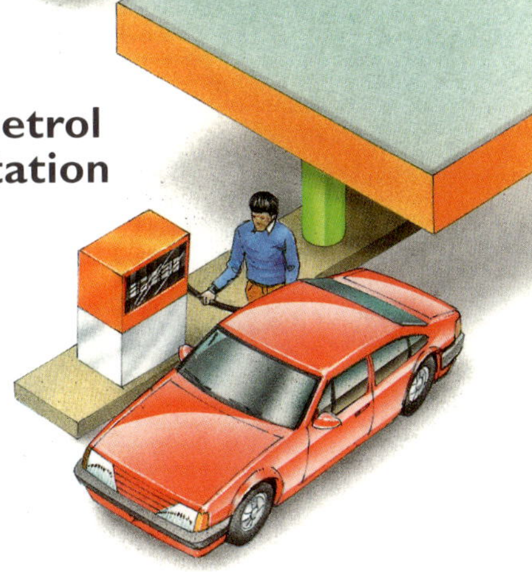

The Sun gives off light energy from 150 million kilometres away. This is known as solar power. It is the source of all the world's energy, and it can be collected directly by solar panels. These turn solar energy into electricity.

What a shower!
We can save energy in the home by not wasting electricity or gas. Heating water takes up energy, and a shower uses less hot water than a bath. So when we shower, we save energy.

Electricity

Imagine what life would be like without the form of energy called electricity. You would not be able to make light or heat by flicking on a switch, and most of the machines in your home would not work!

The electricity we use at home flows through wires. We call this flow an electric current. When you turn on a light switch, a current flows to the bulb and makes it work.

Most electricity we use at home is made in power stations. There, fuel such as coal or oil is burned. The heat energy is used to turn a generator, which makes electricity.

◁ **Another form of electricity** does not flow through wires. It is usually still, or "static". Static electricity from a special generator can make your hair stand on end! You may have noticed this sometimes when your hair is combed quickly, especially on a cold, dry day.

New Words

amber A hard yellow substance from the sap of ancient conifer trees.

current The flow of electricity along a wire.

power station A building where electricity is produced.

static Still, not flowing as an electric current.

charge Electricity that has been stored up.

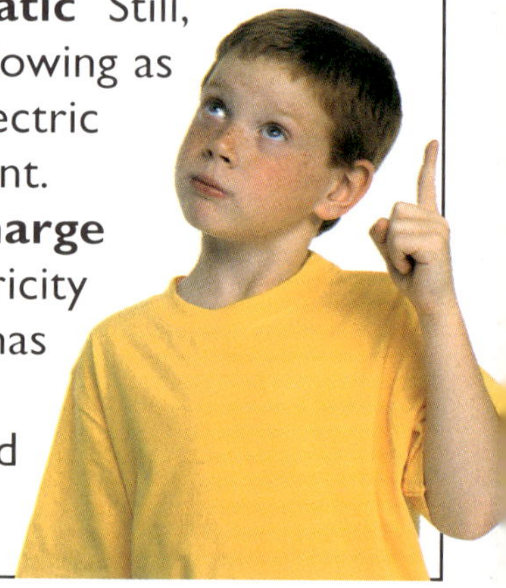

Batteries make and store small amounts of electricity. They are useful because you can carry them around. A car battery is very big. A torch battery is smaller. The battery in a watch is tiny.

WARNING!

Never touch or play with plugs, sockets, wires or any other form of electricity. You will get an electric shock and this could kill you.

A flash of lightning makes a booming noise – thunder. We always hear this after we see the flash, because light travels much faster than sound.

An ancient Greek scientist called Thales discovered static electricity over 2,500 years ago, when he rubbed a piece of amber with a cloth.

△ **Lightning** is a form of static electricity. The electricity builds up inside storm clouds, and then jumps from cloud to cloud or from the cloud to the ground as brilliant flashes of lightning.

STATIC BALLOONS

Blow up a balloon and rub it up and down on a shirt. The rubbing makes static electricity on the plastic skin of the balloon. Hold the balloon against your clothes and let go. The static electricity will stick it there. You can also use the static to pick up small pieces of tissue paper. What happens when the static charge wears off?

The American scientist and statesman, Benjamin Franklin, found out in 1752 that lightning is electricity. He did a famous and extremely dangerous experiment by flying a kite into a thunder cloud.

Magnets

A magnet pulls metal objects such as nails towards itself, with a power called magnetism.

Every magnet has two ends, called its north and south poles. The north pole of one magnet pulls the south pole of another towards it. This is useful in magnetic compasses, which we use to find our way around the world.

The Earth itself is a giant magnet, with strong forces at the two Poles at the top and bottom of the planet.

Magnets are very useful in other ways too, from picking up cars to keeping fridge doors closed.

△ **The metal objects** above are all magnetic. If you put a magnet nearby, they would move towards it. Objects made of wood, plastic and other materials are not magnetic. You could collect your own group of small objects and try them out with a magnet.

Make sure that you keep magnets well away from videos, cassette tapes and computer disks. The effects of magnetism could damage them.

New Words

compass A device with a magnetic pointer that points north, to show people direction.

electromagnet A piece of metal that is made magnetic by electricity.

magnetism The pulling power of magnets.

◁ **Huge magnets** are used in scrapyards to move chunks of scrap metal around. The crane has an electromagnet, which only works when the electricity is switched on. Whenever the crane driver switches it off, the metal drops from the magnet.

When electricity flows along a wire, it makes the wire magnetic. An electromagnet is made by winding a wire around iron and passing electricity through it. Electromagnets are very powerful magnets.

FLOATING COMPASS

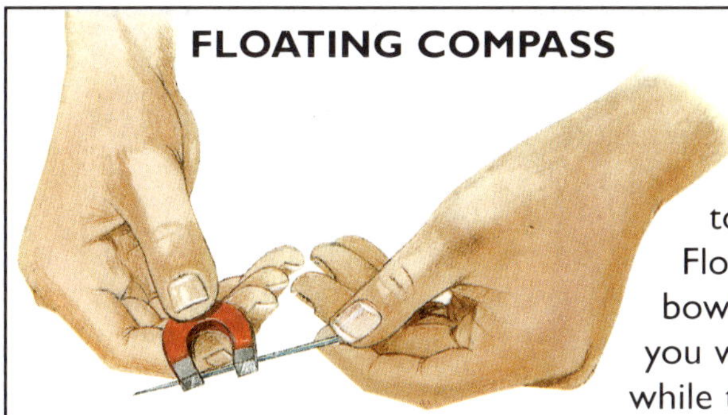

Stroke a needle with a magnet about 50 times. Stroke in the same direction each time, to make the needle magnetic. Then tape the needle to a piece of cork. Float the cork in a bowl of water, and you will see after a while that the needle settles and always points in one direction. This direction is north.

MAGNETIC POLES

Try putting two magnets near each other.

Same poles (north and north, or south and south) will repel each other.

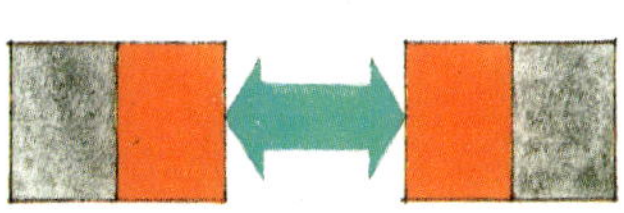

Different poles (north and south) attract each other.

▷ **A compass** helps people find their way. The compass needle is a tiny magnet, and it will always point north, towards North Pole. Line up the needle with the letter N (north) to see where east (E), west (W) and south (S) lie. Compasses are used on ships, planes and land.

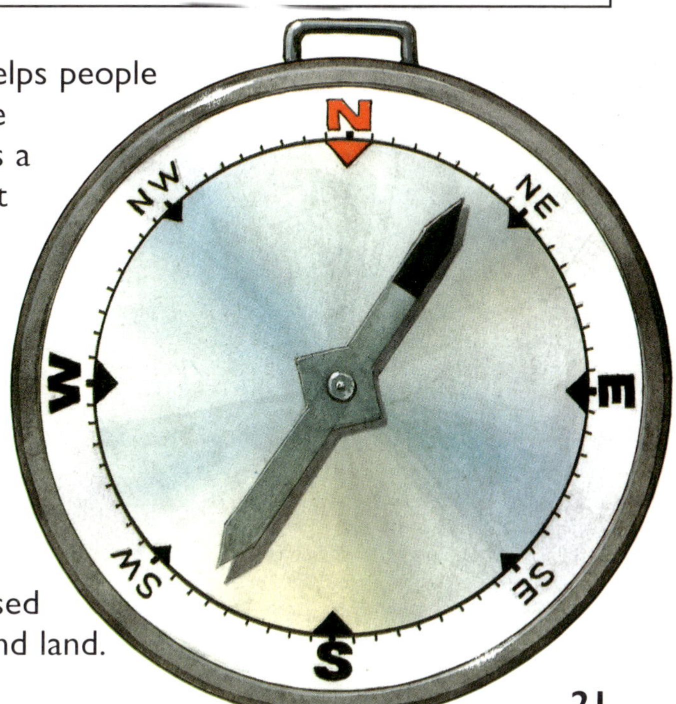

Forces

Forces push or pull things. By doing this, they make things move or stop moving.

Forces can make things start or stop, speed up or slow down, change direction, bend or twist. You put a pushing force on the pedals of your bike when you ride it, and the chain and wheels change this force to one that moves the bike along the road.

Everything that moves has a force acting on it. So without forces nothing much would ever happen!

▽ **The force of gravity** pulls everything down to Earth. If you drop a ball, it falls to the ground. If you throw it up in the air, it will always turn and drop back down.

▽ **A tug of war** is a battle of pulling forces between two sets of human muscles. If the pull on one side of the rope is the same as the pull on the other side, no-one wins. If one team is able to exert greater force, they will pull the other side towards them.

A force called gravity stops us from floating off the planet into space. It also means people on opposite sides of the Earth all stand the right way up.

New Words

crowbar An iron bar used as a simple lever.

friction A rubbing force that holds up sliding forces.

lever A bar that turns on a fixed point, to help us lift or force things open.

pliers A pair of levers, with jaws for gripping things.

△ **A lever** multiplies the force we use to move a weight. A crowbar or pair of pliers works because the further away from your hands the force is used, the bigger it is.

△▽ **Opposite forces** make boats float. Gravity makes the boat's weight pull it down, but water pushes it up. The weight is spread over a large area, so the water has a lot to push on and holds the boat up.

A rubbing action called friction stops things from sliding. When you pedal your bike, you are working against the friction of the road on your tyres. If you ride uphill, you are working against two forces – friction and gravity.

SPINNING COLOURS

Here's a way to mix the colours of the rainbow back together. Divide a card disk into seven equal sections. Colour the sections with the seven colours of the rainbow. Push a sharpened pencil through the middle of the disc and spin it fast on the pencil point. The colours will all mix back to a greyish white.

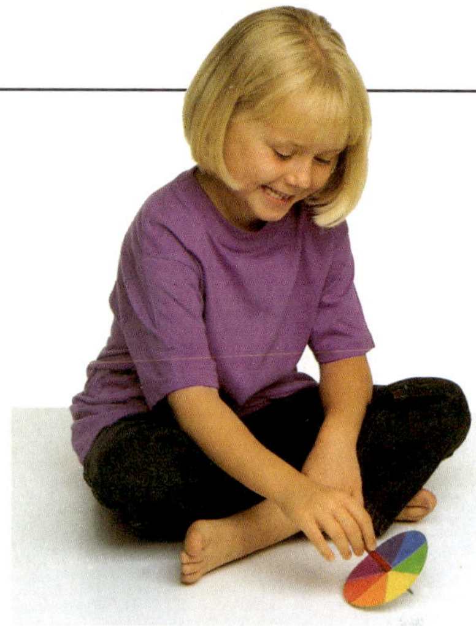

◁ **Light bounces off** still water in the same way that it bounces back to you from a mirror. The image that we see in the water or in a mirror is called a reflection.

Shadows are dark shapes. They are made when something gets in the way of light and blocks it out. This happens because light travels in straight lines and cannot bend around corners.

NEW WORDS

lens A curved piece of glass or plastic that is used to change the direction of light.

prism A triangular piece of glass that breaks up the colours of light.

reflection The image of something that is seen in a mirror or another reflecting surface.

triangular Having three sides, like a triangle.

In this book, all the colours you see are made of a mixture of just four coloured printing inks – blue, red, yellow and black.

▷ **If you pass a beam of light** through a triangular piece of glass, called a prism, the light gets split up into its different colours, just like a rainbow. The band of rainbow colours is called the spectrum of light.

Light and Colour

Light is the fastest moving form of energy there is. Sunlight travels to Earth through space as light waves. We see things when light from them travels to our eyes.

Light seems to us to be colourless, but really it is a mixture of colours. These are soaked up differently by various objects. A banana lets yellow bounce off it and soaks up the other colours, so the banana looks yellow.

△ **Light normally travels** in straight lines. The plastic lenses in glasses change the direction of light and help people who need them to see things more clearly.

△ **The curved lens** in a magnifying glass also bends light, making things look bigger. You can move the position of the glass, to see things the size you want.

◁ **A rainbow** shows sunlight in seven different colours. This happens when sunlight passes through raindrops and gets split up. Starting with the outer circle, the colours of a rainbow are red, orange, yellow, green, blue, indigo and violet. The colours are always in the same order.

Sound

All sounds are made by things vibrating, or moving backwards and forwards very quickly. Sounds travel through the air in waves.

Our ears pick up sound waves travelling in the air around us. Sounds can move through other gases too, as well as through liquids and solids. So you can hear sounds when you swim underwater. Astronauts on the Moon, where there is no air, cannot speak to each other directly and have to use radio.

LOUD AND QUIET

Bigger vibrations make bigger sound waves and sound louder. We measure loudness in decibels. Leaves falling gently on the ground might make 10 decibels of noise. A jet plane taking off makes about 120 decibels.

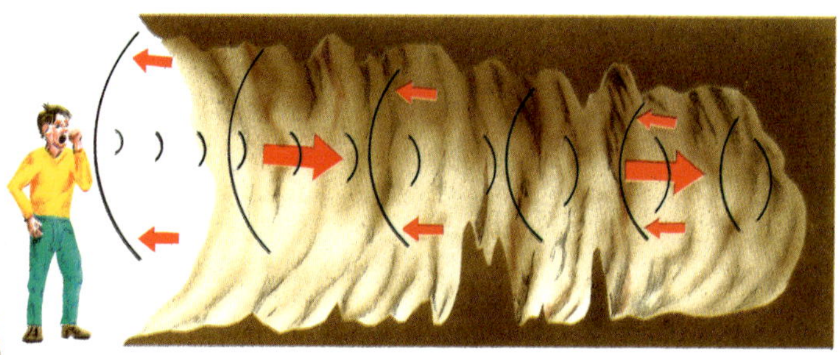

◁ **Sometimes sound waves** bounce back to you off a hard surface. When this happens, the sound makes an echo. A cave or a long corridor are good places to make an echo.

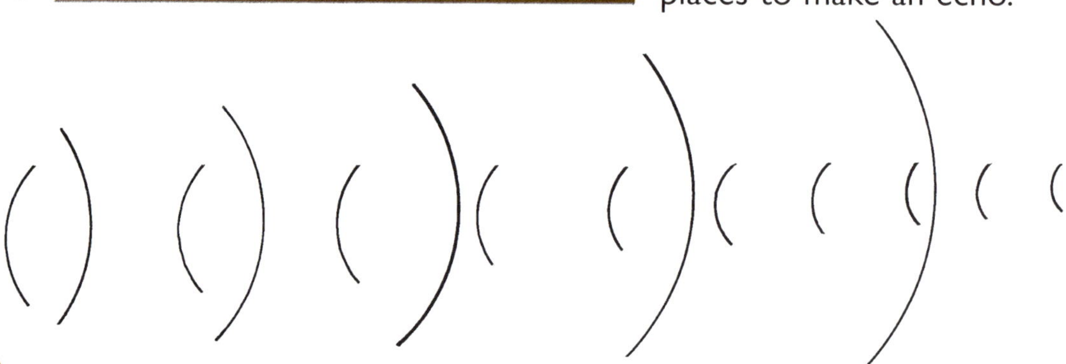

◁ **When you pluck a guitar string,** it vibrates very fast and makes sound waves. If you put your finger gently on a plucked string, you will be able to feel it vibrating. If you press down hard on the string and stop the vibration, you will also stop the sound.

Sound moves at a speed of about 1,225 kilometres an hour. That's 30 times quicker than the fastest human runner, but almost a million times slower than the speed of light! A Concorde supersonic jet can fly at twice the speed of sound.

HIGH AND LOW

A big horn makes lower sounds than a high-pitched whistle. A big cat makes a booming roar, while a mouse makes a high-pitched squeak. That's because they make different vibrations. The quicker something vibrates, the higher the sound it makes.

whistle

horn

tiger

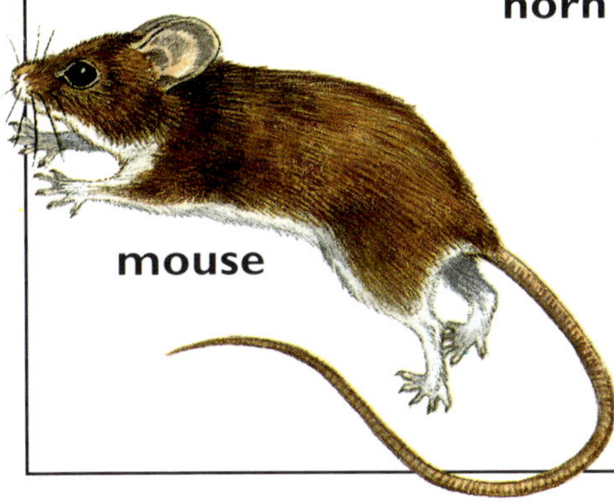
mouse

New Words

decibel A unit that is used to measure the loudness of sounds.

echo A sound that is heard again when it bounces back off something.

vibrate To move very quickly back and forth.

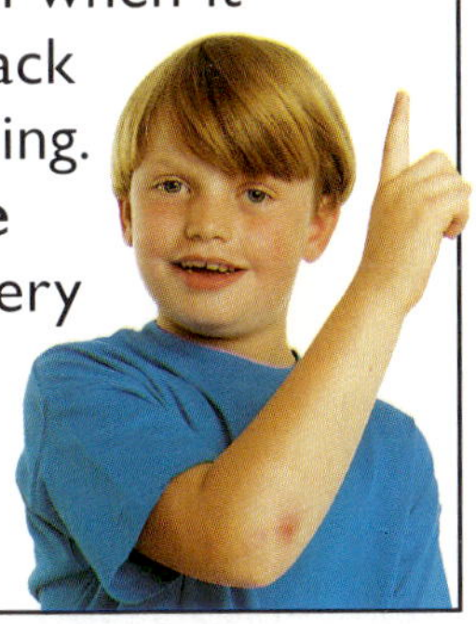

◁ **The vibrations** made by guitar strings travel through the air as sound waves. They do this by making the air vibrate as well. Sometimes people put a hand to their ear to try and collect more sounds.

Dogs can hear both lower and higher sounds than people can. Bats and dolphins can make and hear even higher-pitched sounds, and they use this ability to find their way around.

Why wear ear muffs?
People who work with loud machines wear muffs to protect their hearing. This is because loud noises are painful to the ears and can damage them, especially if the noise goes on for a long time.

Cars and Bikes

Today's cars come in all shapes and sizes, from small city cars to big luxury vehicles. Most of them are powered by engines that run on petrol or diesel oil.

To save energy and cut down on the pollution caused by exhaust fumes, new types of engines are being invented. Cars are also being made safer all the time.

Motorbikes take up less room on the road. Cycles use just human energy to power them along.

▽ **This car** runs on the Sun's energy. Its flat shape helps solar panels to collect the energy. One day cars like this may drive on our roads and motorways.

Most cars are built by robots. In the factory, they weld different parts together as car bodies move between them.

▷ **Motorcycle racing** is a popular sport. Riders lean over as they take bends at great speed. This helps them keep their balance and go faster. The fastest motorbikes go at over 200 kilometres per hour.

△ **Mountain bikes** are strong and fast. They are built for riding on rough tracks, but are very popular on city roads too. As more cars make more traffic jams, cycling becomes even more popular.

Your bike's gears allow you to ride slowly or more quickly while you pedal at a comfortable rate. A car's gears do the same job for the engine, by changing the speed of the wheels.

▽ **In most cars,** the engine is at the front, under the bonnet. It burns petrol, to turn a shaft connected to the wheels. The car's battery stores electricity, and the radiator helps to cool the engine.

New Words

diesel A fuel made from oil that is used to power engines.

exhaust The waste gases produced and given off by an engine.

gears A set of toothed wheels that change the speed of a car's or bike's wheels.

weld To join pieces of metal or plastic together by heating them and pressing or hammering.

robots Machines which are programmed to work in a similar way to humans. They are useful for doing repetitive tasks.

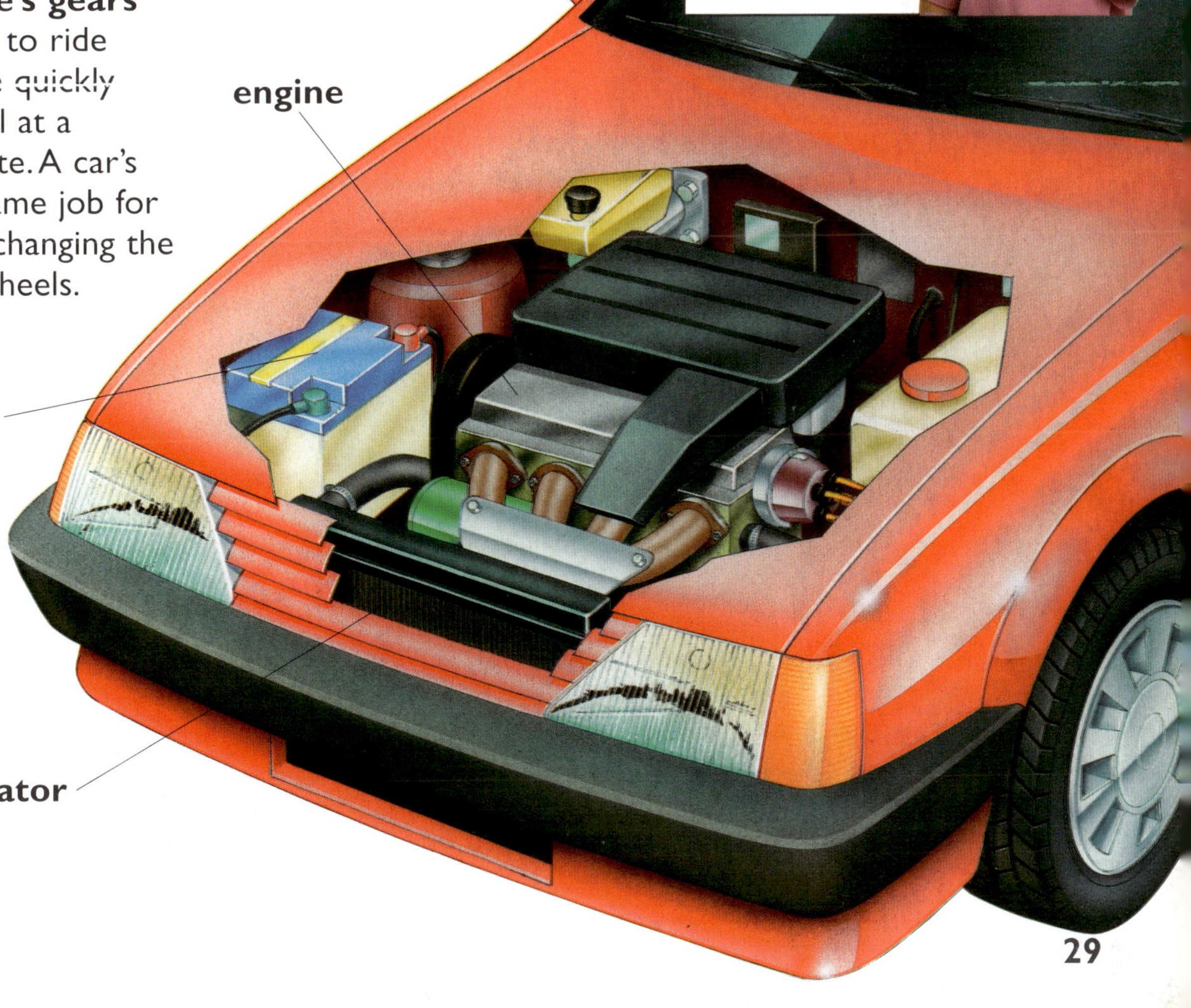

Trains, Ships and Planes

What is a maglev train?
Maglev stands for magnetic levitation. A maglev train floats on a magnetic field and is driven by the effect of magnets. It has no wheels and travels along a guideway instead of on rails. Maglevs may well be the trains of the future.

Trains carry people and goods in carriages and wagons. They are pulled along their railways by powerful locomotives.

△ **Helicopters** use high-speed spinning blades to fly in any direction. Unlike planes, they can hover in mid-air. They can also land on small helipads on top of tall buildings, lighthouses or oil rigs out at sea.

Ships have sailed on the world's oceans and seas for thousands of years. Hundreds of years ago they helped people to explore new lands and settle in other parts of the world.

More recently, ships have been overtaken by jet planes as the quickest and cheapest form of long-distance transport.

Some modern ships have water-jets instead of propellers to push them along. The jets drive water out at great pressure and can be turned to steer the ship too.

◁ **The steam engine "The Rocket"** won a railway competition in 1829. It used coal to heat water and make steam. The steam in its boiler drove two big cylinders, which turned the front wheels.

▷ **Steam locomotives** pulled most trains for 150 years, and some are still running. Railway engineers built long bridges across rivers and valleys, and bored tunnels underground and through mountains.

▷ **Concorde**, the world's only supersonic passenger plane, flies at almost twice the speed of sound, but is noisier than most planes. A Concorde can carry less than a quarter of the number of passengers that a huge jumbo jet can manage.

New Words

engineer An expert who plans, designs and helps to build things.

helipad A small landing place specially built for a helicopter.

maglev Magnetic levitation, floating in the air on magnets.

propeller A set of spinning blades that push a ship along through the water.

Oil supertankers are the biggest ships in the world. The largest of all is 458 metres long.

△ **Some cargo ships** are huge and can carry heavier goods than planes. They often transport the goods in containers that are all the same size.

◁ **Electric trains** collect electricity from an extra rail. This can be on the ground or on overhead cables. New electric trains are more comfortable and quieter than diesel trains.

▷ **In Japan,** millions of people travel on fast "bullet" trains as they speed to work in big cities. French high-speed trains, called TGVs, are even faster. They hold the world speed record for trains: 515 km/h!

bullet train

Technology in the Home

Today most people have a lot of helpful machines in their homes. The machines are there to make life easier and to save people time. Most of them are powered by electricity.

Housework is much easier now than it has ever been. Before people had washing machines, they would take hours washing their clothes by hand. Now they just spend a few minutes filling the machine and setting the right wash programme.

Home technology means that people have more time – to work or to relax.

◁ **A microwave oven** cooks food very quickly. It does this by sending invisible waves of energy, called microwaves, into the food. This makes the watery parts of the food vibrate and get hot.

New Words

microwave A small wave of energy used in a microwave oven to heat food quickly.

technology The use or the study of machines.

vacuum cleaner A machine that sucks up dirt and collects it in a bag.

▷ **A washing machine** is really quite a simple electrical device. It works by mixing dirty clothes up with soapy water. A drum inside the machine turns to slosh the clothes in the water, and then clean water rinses away the soap and dirt. Finally, the machine's drum spins very fast, to help dry the clothes.

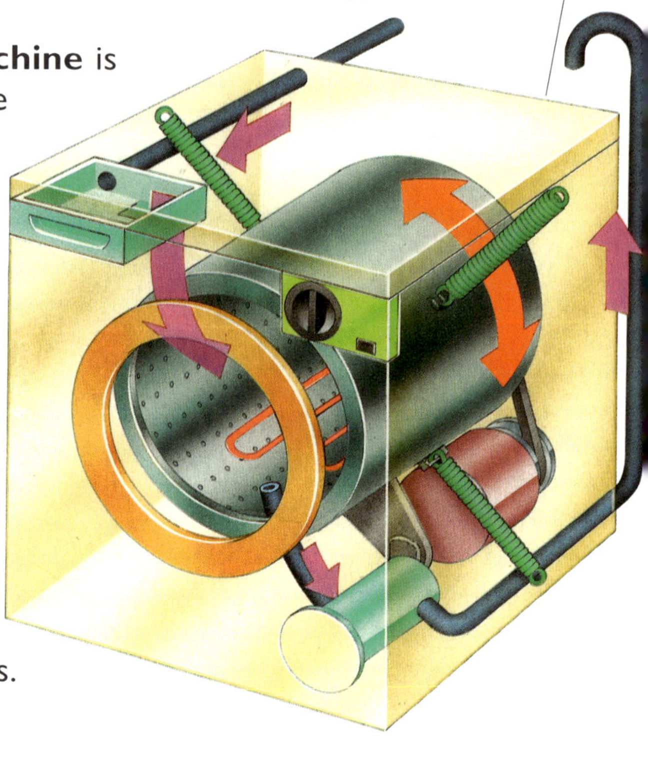

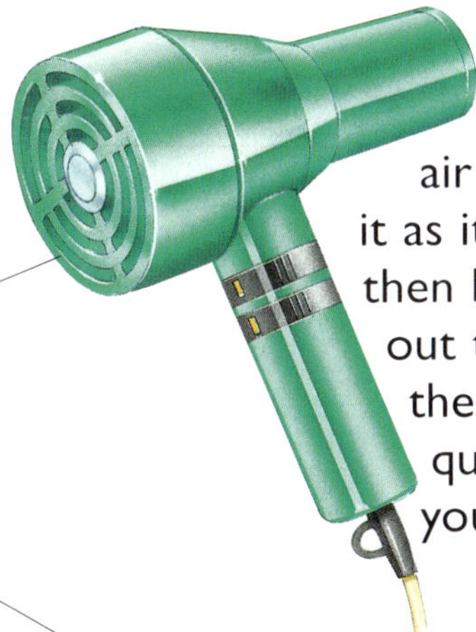

◁ **A hairdryer** sucks air in at the back, warms it as it passes through, and then blows the warm air out through the nozzle at the front. This is much quicker than waiting for your hair to dry.

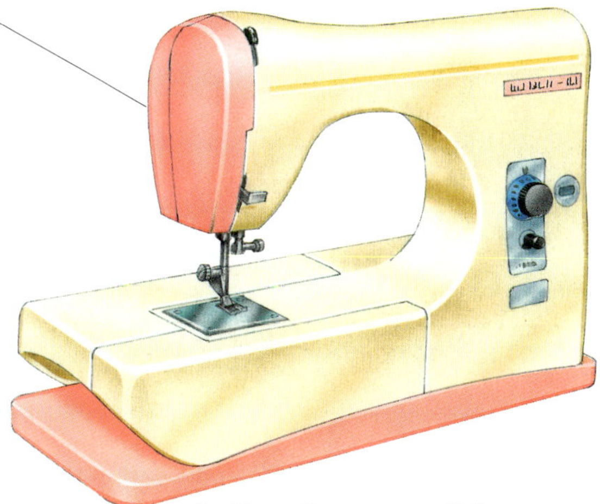

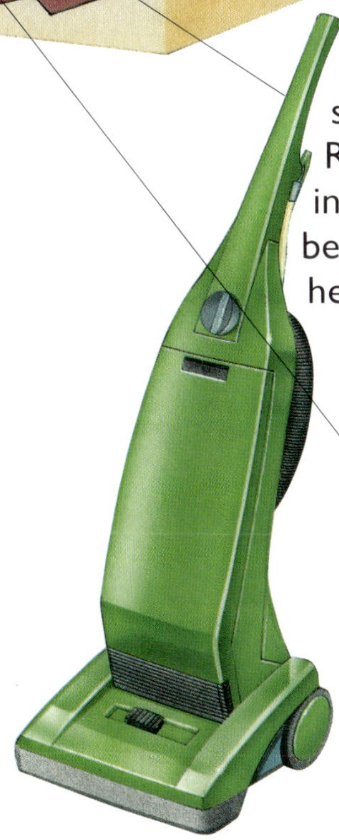

◁ **A vacuum cleaner** sucks up dust and dirt. Rushing air carries them into a bag, which can then be emptied. Brushes usually help loosen the dust.

△ **Sewing machines** were some of the earliest machines in the home. But in the old days they were powered by human effort rather than electricity. The person sewing pushed a pedal back and forth with her feet, to make the needle go up and down. Now an electric motor does all the hard work.

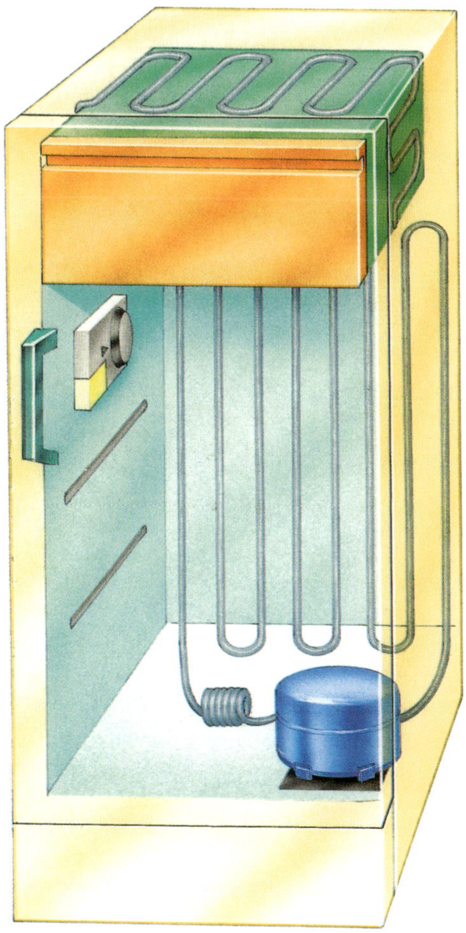

▷ **A refrigerator,** or fridge, keeps food cold by removing heat from inside the cabinet. A liquid flows around pipes at the back of the fridge. The liquid changes to a gas and takes up heat from inside the cabinet. The pipes give off the heat behind the fridge.

Many machines were originally American. The Electric Suction Sweeper Company produced the world's first vacuum cleaners in the USA in 1908. Two years later, the head of the company, William Hoover, renamed it the Hoover Company. Vacuum cleaners are still called "Hoovers" today.

Computers

Computers can do all sorts of different jobs for us, easily and very quickly. Many people use computers at home, as well as at work and at school.

We can use computers to write letters and reports; or to store lots of information, such as lists or addresses; or to do complicated sums; or to design things.

Most of the work you do on a computer can be seen on its screen. If you want to, you can also print work out on paper.

▽ **You can use a keyboard** and a mouse to put information into the computer. Then you can store your work on a disk, as well as inside the computer itself.

What is E-mail?
It stands for electronic mail, a way of sending messages between computers all over the world. You write a letter on your computer, then send it down a telephone line to someone else's computer, instantly. In comparison, ordinary post is so slow that E-mailers call it "snail mail".

STRINGING ALONG
To create your own phone system, make a hole in the bottom of two plastic or paper cups, or yoghurt pots. Then thread a long piece of string through the holes and tie a knot at each end, inside the cup. Ask a friend to pull the string tight and put a cup to his ear. Now speak into your cup and he will hear you. It's as fast as E-mail!

▷ **There are lots** of exciting computer games. You play many of them by using a joystick.

NEW WORDS

disk A small piece of plastic that stores computer information.

joystick A device with a moving handle that is used to put information into a computer.

keyboard A set of keys used to type information.

mouse A control unit you can move and click to put information into a computer.

▽ **When you put on** a virtual-reality headset, you enter a pretend world created by a computer. Inside the headset are two small screens, showing you pictures that look real. If you use a special glove to touch things, the computer reacts to every move you make. This picture shows how the system could be used to control planes. An air traffic controller could see the planes as if they were real and give commands to tell them what to do.

TV and Radio

Many people spend hours each day watching TV or listening to radio. Along with newspapers and magazines, TV and radio provide us with entertainment and information.

Television signals can be received by an aerial or by a satellite dish. Some people have TV signals brought straight into their homes through a cable. In most countries there are many different channels and programmes to choose from, day and night.

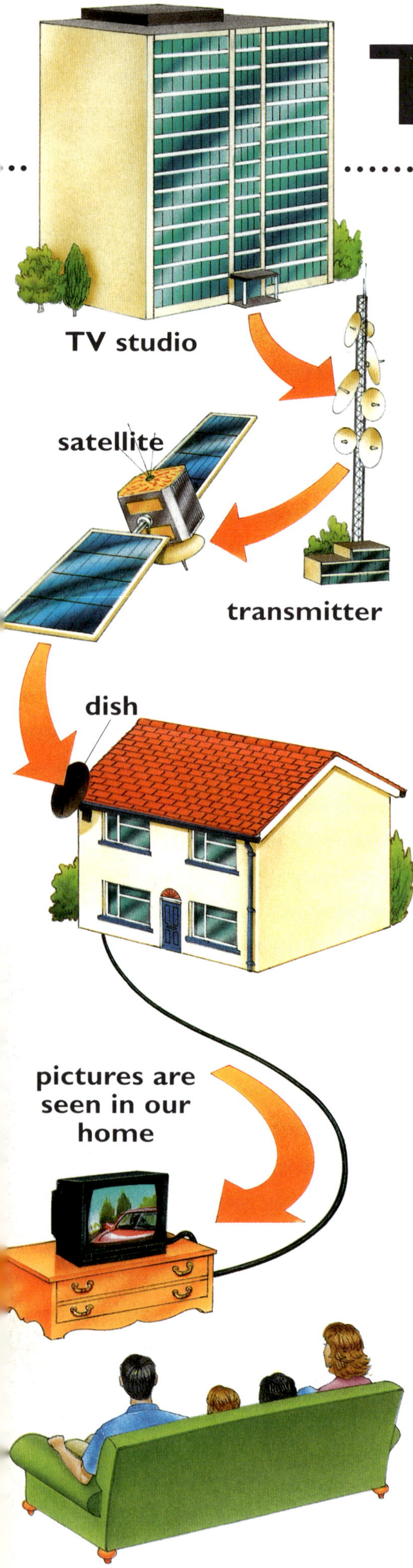

◁ **For satellite TV**, a programme is transmitted to a satellite in space. The signal is then beamed back to Earth by the satellite and is picked up by dishes on people's homes. Their television set changes the signal back into pictures.

△ **Working in a TV studio,** cameramen use video cameras to record programmes. These are bigger, more complicated versions of the camcorders that people use at home. Many different technicians work in TV and radio.

▽ **The leaves** and flowers of water lilies float on the surface of the water. We call these lily pads. The plants' stems are under the water, and their roots are in the mud and soil at the bottom of the pond.

▷ **Some bromeliads** live on other plants, in the rainforest. They grow in pockets of soil that form in the bark of trees. Their roots dangle freely and take in most of their moisture from the damp forest air.

The largest leaves of any plant grow on palm trees on islands in the Indian Ocean. The leaves are up to 20 metres long. The pads of some large water lilies grow over 2 metres across.

▽ **Leaves** take in carbon dioxide gas through tiny holes on their underside. They also give out oxygen, which is why plants are so important to all other living creatures, including us.

△ **Cacti** live in hot, dry regions, such as deserts. They store water in their fleshy stems. Their leaves are in the shape of sharp spines, which help protect them from desert animals.

New Words

carbon dioxide A gas used by plants to make their food; it is also the waste gas that we breathe out.

chlorophyll A green substance in plants, which they use to trap sunlight.

photosynthesis The process that plants use to make food, using sunlight and carbon dioxide and giving off oxygen.

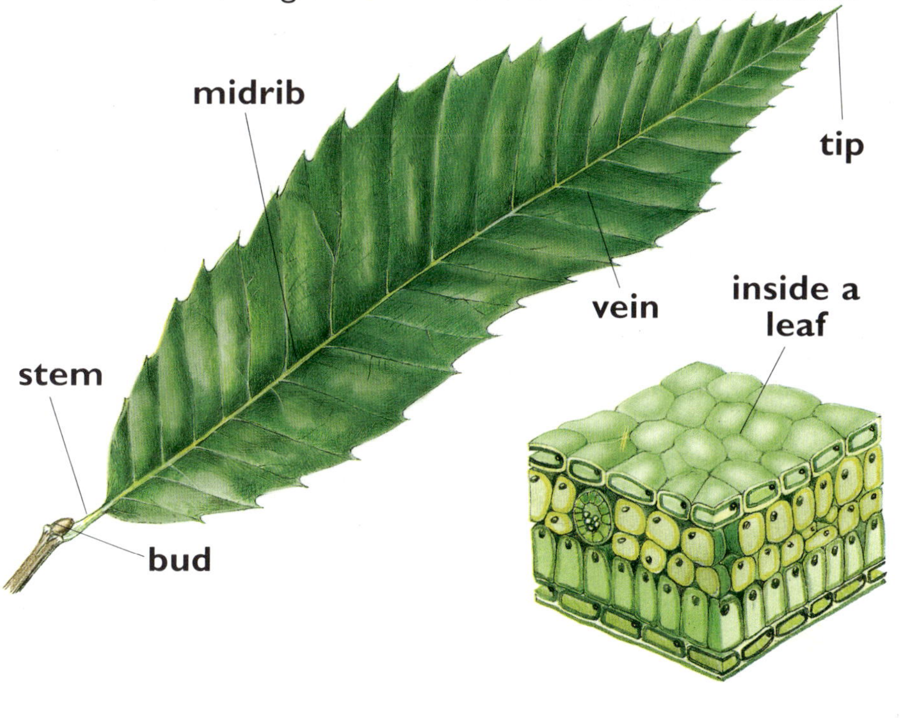

△ **A TV set** receives electrical signals, which it changes into pictures. It fires streams of particles onto the back of the screen. They build up a picture, and this changes many times each second.

What does television mean?
"Tele" means far, so television simply means "far sight". When we watch TV, we are seeing things that are far away. A telescope is a "far-seeing instrument", and a telephone is a "far sound"!

New Words

aerial A metal device that receives and sends TV and radio signals.

satellite dish A round aerial that receives TV signals bounced back from a satellite in space.

signal A series of radio waves that can make up pictures and sounds.

transmitter A device, usually a tall pole, that sends out radio and television signals.

South Korea makes more colour television sets than any other country: over 16 million every year!

▽ **A radio telescope** is used to send and receive radio waves. Both radio and TV signals travel as radio waves. Astronomers also use radio telescopes to pick up signals from parts of space that we can't see through other telescopes.

The largest radio telescope in the world is at Arecibo, on the Caribbean island of Puerto Rico. The dish is 305 metres across and stands inside a circle of hills.

The world's first radio broadcast was made in the USA in 1906. The first proper TV service began in 1936 in London. At that time there were just 100 television sets in the whole of the UK!

Plants

Living plants are found almost everywhere on Earth where there is sunlight, warmth and water. They use these to make their own food.

Plants have a special way of using the Sun's energy, with a green substance in their leaves called chlorophyll. They take in a gas called carbon dioxide from the air and mix it with water and minerals from the soil. In this way they make a form of sugar, which is their food. This whole process is called photosynthesis.

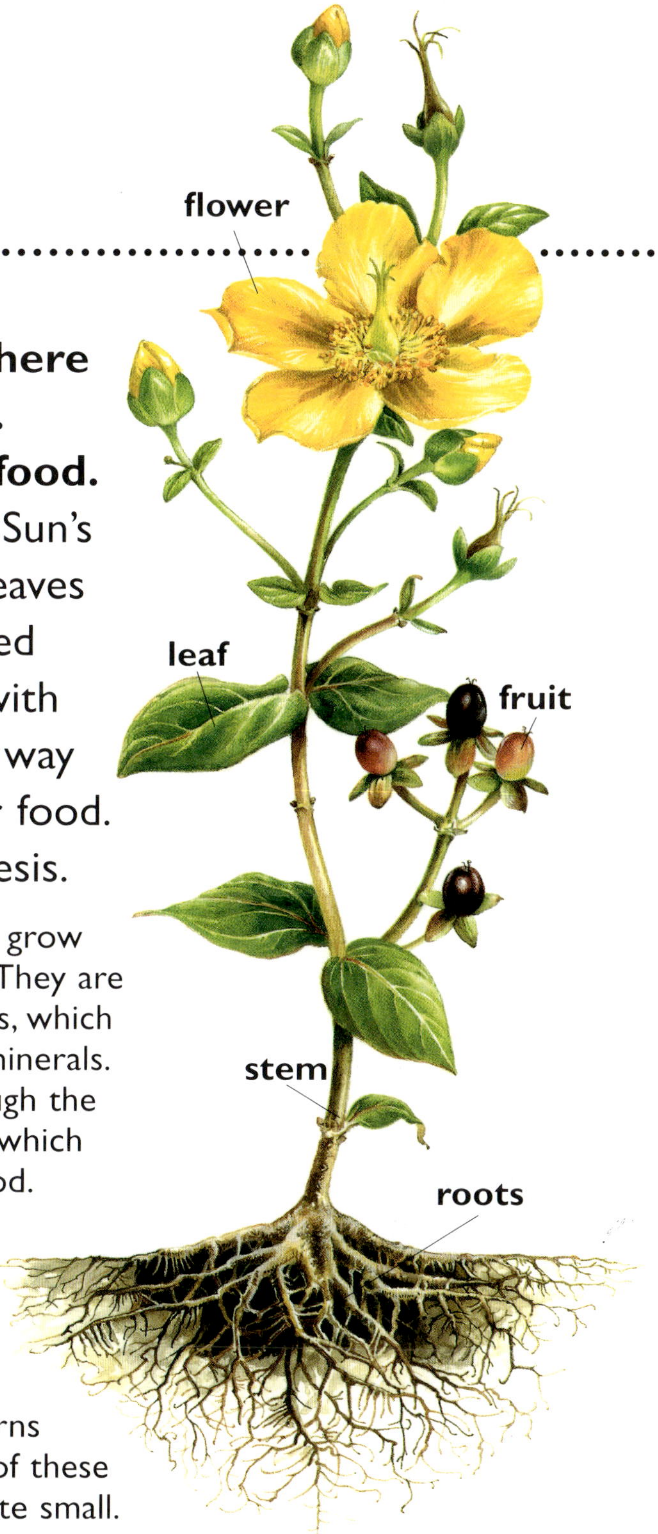

▷ **A plant's roots** grow down into the soil. They are covered in tiny hairs, which take in water and minerals. Water moves through the stem to the leaves, which make the plant's food.

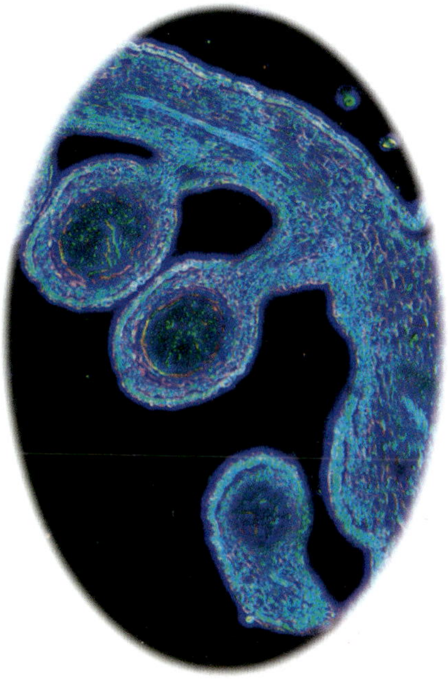

◁ **Part of a fern** seen through a microscope. There are about 10,000 different kinds of ferns in the world. Most of these green plants are quite small.

SUN BLOCK

Cover a patch of green grass with an old tin or saucer – but not on someone's prize lawn! Lift the tin after a few days and you will see that the grass is losing its colour. After a week, it will be very pale.
This is because it couldn't make food in the dark. Take the tin away and the grass will soon recover.

Flowers

People grow flowers so that they can enjoy their colours, shapes and perfume. But flowers are more than just pretty. They have an important job to do for their plants.

Flowers make the seeds that grow into new plants. Male parts of the flower produce pollen grains. When these reach the female parts, they fertilize eggs, to make seeds. Birds, insects and other animals often help this process by feeding on flowers and moving the pollen grains. This process is called pollination.

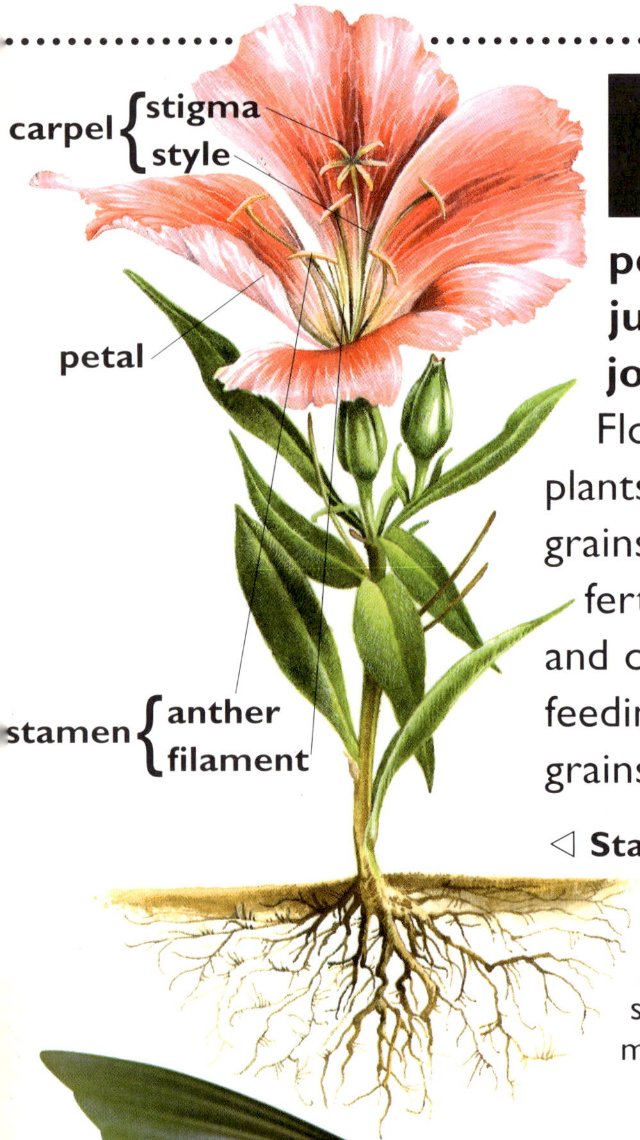

◁ **Stamens** are male parts of a flower. The stigma at the top of the female carpel catches pollen grains, which reach down the style to meet egg cells and make seeds.

△ **A hummingbird** can hover in front of a flower while it feeds on the sweet nectar. Pollen sticks to its long beak and is carried to the female part of the plant or to another plant when the bird next feeds. The same thing happens with bees, when they collect nectar to make honey.

▽ **Some plants** have many small flowers arranged on one stem, while others have one big flower at the top. The petals do not usually last long. Once they have done their job and attracted animals to pollinate the plant, they begin to drop off.

▽ **There are almost** 20,000 different types of orchid. Some grow on the ground, and others grow on the branches of trees. Their seeds are as light as dust and are known to have been blown over 1,000 kilometres by the wind.

△ **It is easy to see** how beautiful, colourful flowers attract insects and other animals. Many flowers can be found in all sorts of different colours. There are more than 200 different types of chrysanthemums, which are very popular with gardeners.

NEW WORDS

- **carpel** The female parts of a flower.
- **nectar** A sweet liquid produced by flowers and collected by bees and other animals for food.
- **petal** The outer, coloured part of a flower.
- **pollen** Powder produced by male parts of a flower, containing male cells for making seeds.
- **stamen** The male part of a flower, where pollen is made.

Bees are the best-known collectors of nectar. They find flowers by their colour and their scent. Some bats also feed on nectar, in the same way as hummingbirds. The bats have long, tube-like tongues.

▷ **Some trees**, such as birch and hazel, have flowers that hang down like loose tassels. These flowers, called catkins, often appear before the tree's leaves each spring. The pollen on the catkins is easily blown by the wind, so that it moves from flower to flower and tree to tree.

Trees

Trees are not only among the largest living things on Earth, but also can live the longest.

A trunk is really just a hard, woody stem. Under the protective bark, water and food travel up through the outer layer of wood, called the sapwod, to the tree's crown of branches and leaves.

Fine roots take in the water, but trees have big, strong roots as well. These will help anchor the trees very firmly in the ground.

New Words

cone The cone-shaped fruit of conifer trees, containing the trees' seeds.

forester A person who works in and looks after a fore wood.

heartw The centra of hard wo in a tree trunk.

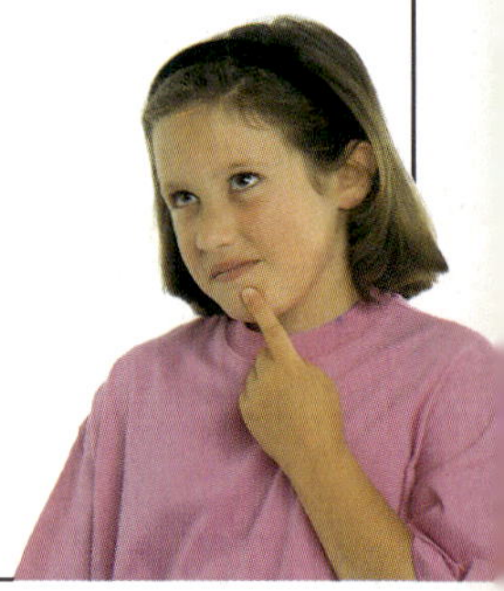

The oldest living trees on Earth are bristlecone pines in the USA. Some are over 5,000 years old.

Mangrove trees grow in swamps. They are the only trees that live in salty water.

▽ **Different leaves** do different jobs. Small leaves, like those on fir trees or cacti, lose less water than broad, flat leaves. Big leaves show a larger surface area to the Sun and so are able to make more food.

△ **The beautiful leaves** of the tamarind, an evergreen tree that grows in warm regions of the world. It can grow to a height of 24 metres.

▽ **The leaves of birch trees** are shaped like triangles, with toothed edges. In the autumn, they turn brown before falling from the tree. Native Americans used the bark of birch trees to make canoes.

◁ **As an oak tree grows** and the trunk widens, its bark breaks up into pieces like a jigsaw. In the middle of the trunk is a core of dark brown heartwood.

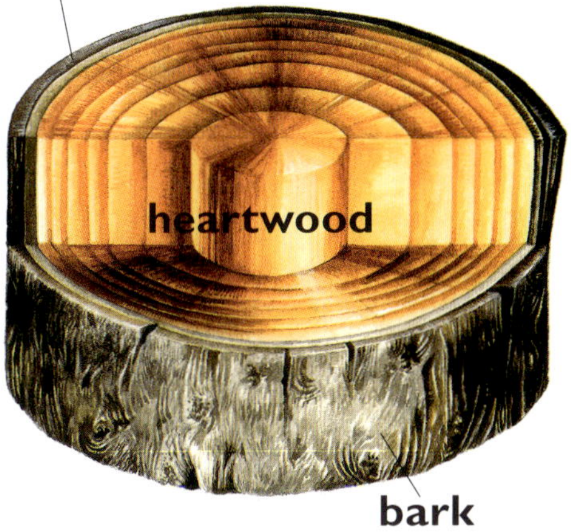

△ **Trees grow** a new ring of wood every year. If there is lots of sunshine and rainfall, that year's ring is wide. Foresters count the rings of felled trees to see how old they are.

Many palm trees have no branches. Instead, they have large, fan-shaped leaves that grow straight out from the top of the trunk. Palms grow best in parts of the world where it is warm all year round.

BARK PATTERNS

Every tree has a unique pattern on its bark. You can see these wonderful patterns by transferring them to paper. Just attach or hold a sheet of paper firmly against a tree trunk. Then carefully rub over the paper with a crayon until the bark pattern shows up. Bark rubbings make beautiful pictures, and you can use different coloured crayons to make unusual effects.

Fruit, Nuts and Seeds

△ **Cherries** are small fruits surrounding a hard stone that contains a seed.

A fruit is the part of a plant that protects and feeds new seeds as they grow. Berries and nuts are really different kinds of fruits.

Hard shells grow around seeds that will fall to the ground. Soft fruits are often eaten by animals. When a bird eats berries, the seeds usually pass through the bird's digestive system without being harmed. So without knowing it, the bird may later deposit the seeds in ground a long way away.

Some other fruits are very light and are blown by the wind.

△ **The pips in apples** are the seeds. Fleshy fruits are juicy and good to eat. This makes them attractive to animals, which help spread the seeds. We grow apple trees specially for their fruit, and carefully plant the seeds ourselves.

▷ **Nectarines** are a type of peach. Each nectarine has a large, hard seed, which we call the stone. Cherries and plums also have stones.

The world's largest seeds are produced by coco-de-mer trees. Each of the huge heart-shaped seeds can weigh as much as 20 kilos.

◁ **It's easy to see** the cluster of seeds inside these juicy melons. Melons are specially grown in warm countries for their fruit.

GROW WATERCRESS

Wild cress grows in streams or on mud. You can easily grow cress seeds yourself in compost, or even on paper! In a tray, place a 3 cm-layer of seed compost, or two sheets of kitchen roll, and wet this thoroughly. Put the tray on a window sill and always keep it damp. In about 7 to 10 days you will be able to cut your cress and make yourself a tasty sandwich.

▽ **The European hazel tree** grows up to 12 metres tall. It flowers in early spring, before the leaves come out, and then produces small, hard hazelnuts.

▷ **Walnut trees** are very useful to people. They give us the wrinkled fruits we call walnuts, and the tree's timber is used for furniture.

New Words

digestive system The part of the body through which food passes.

fruit The part of a plant that protects and feeds new seeds as they grow.

shell The hard outer part of a nut.

◁ **Coconuts** are the fruit of the coconut palm. They can float, and so can be carried long distances by the sea, to land and take root on a faraway beach.

The watery liquid inside coconuts is called coconut milk. It makes a refreshing drink.

Quiz

1. What are scientists' tests called? *(page 8)*

2. What can you use to see things more clearly and closer up? *(page 9)*

3. How long does it take for the Earth to travel around the Sun? *(page 10)*

4. How many trips around the Earth does the Moon take in a year? *(page 11)*

5. What material was Cinderella's shoe made of? *(page 12)*

6. Which material comes from a Greek word meaning "fit for moulding". *(page 13)*

7. What does a liquid take the shape of? *(page 14)*

8. What happens to ice cubes when you heat them? *(page 15)*

9. Where do all living things get their energy from? *(page 16)*

10. Which uses less water, a bath or a shower? *(page 17)*

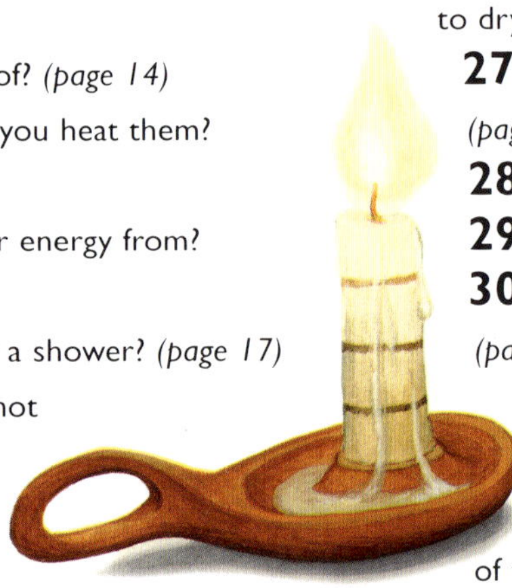

11. Which form of electricity does not flow through wires? *(page 18)*

12. Which comes first, thunder or lightning? *(page 19)*

13. What are the two ends of a magnet called? *(page 20)*

14. Which magnetic instrument helps people find their way? *(page 21)*

15. Which force pulls everything down to Earth? *(page 22)*

16. Which of these is not a lever – crowbar, battery, pliers? *(page 23)*

17. How many sides does a triangle have? *(page 24)*

18. Can you name the colours of the rainbow? *(page 25)*

19. Where are good places to make an echo? *(page 26)*

20. Why do some workmen wear ear muffs? *(page 27)*

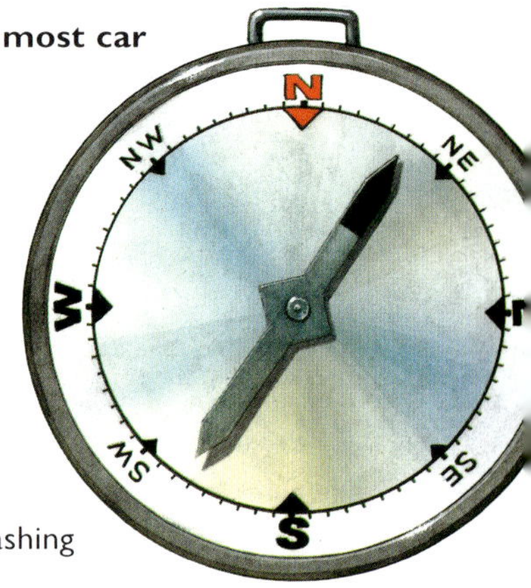

21. What do most car engines run on? *(page 28)*

22. What does a car's radiator do? *(page 29)*

23. What does maglev stand for? *(page 30)*

24. What is the name of the world's only supersonic passenger airliner? *(page 31)*

25. What turns inside a washing machine? *(page 32)*

26. Is it quicker to use a hairdryer or to wait for your hair to dry? *(page 33)*

27. What do you store your computer's work on? *(page 34)*

28. In computing, what is a mouse? *(page 35)*

29. How does satellite television work? *(page 36)*

30. Where is the world's largest radio telescope? *(page 37)*

31. What is carbon dioxide? *(page 38)*

32. What is the name of the green substance in plants? *(page 39)*

33. Which birds hover in front of flowers while feeding? *(page 40)*

34. Which insects are the best-known collectors of nectar? *(page 41)*

35. What do a tree's roots do? *(page 42)*

36. Which trees have no branches? *(page 43)*

37. What are apple pips? *(page 44)*

38. What is the hard, outer part of a nut called? *(page 45)*

Index

Acknowledgements

The publishers wish to thank the following artists who have contributed to this book:

Julie Banyard Page 39 (R), 40 (TL), 43 (TR);
Mike Foster (The Maltings Partnership) 12 (BR), 15 (CR), 17 (B), 27 (BR), 30 (TL), 34 (CL), 37 (TR), caption icons throughout;
Ron Hayward 13 (L), 21 (C), 38 (B), 39 (B);
Mel Pickering (Contour Publishing) 10 (B), 11 (C, CB), 26 (C);
Roger Stewart 11 (T), 20 (L), 21 (BL, BR), 25 (TR, CR), 27 (TC), 30 (C), 31 (BR);
Terry Riley 27 (TL);
Guy Smith (Mainline Design) 15 (BR), 16 (T, B), 17 (R), 18 (BR), 24 (BR), 26 (TR), 29 (TL, BR), 32-33, 34 (C), 36 (L), 37 (TL);
Michael White (Temple Rogers) 22-23 (B).

The publishers wish to thank the following for supplying photographs for this book:

Susanne Bull Page 45 (T);
Honda Dream solar car 28 (T);
Gerard Kelly 43 (B);
Miles Kelly archives 10 (TR), 11 (L, TR), 12 (TR, BL), 13 (TR, BR), 14 (TR, C, B), 15 (T), 18 (BL), 19 (T), 23 (TR, CR), 24 (C), 25 (BL), 26 (L), 27 (TR, TC below), 28 (B), 30 (TR, BR), 31 (TR, CR, CL), 37 (BR), 38 (T, CL, CR), 39 (CL), 40 (TR, B), 41 (T, CL, CR, BR), 42 (C, BL, BR), 43 (TL), 44 (TR, TL, C, B), 45 (CL, CR, B);
Rex Features 36 (CR) /The Times/Simon Walker;
Sega Rally 35 (TR);
The Stock Market 8 (TL, B), 9 (BR), 12 (C), 21 (T);
Science Photo Library 35 (BR) /Geoff Tompkinson.
All model photography by **Mike Perry at David Lipson Photography Ltd.**

Models in this series:
Lisa Anness, Sophie Clark, Alison Cobb, Edward Delaney, Elizabeth Fallas, Ryan French, Luke Gilder, Lauren May Headley, Christie Hooper, Caroline Kelly, Alice McGhee, Daniel Melling, Ryan Oyeyemi, Aaron Phipps, Eriko Sato, Jack Wallace.

Clothes for model photography supplied by:
Adams Children's Wear